D0458142

Unsolved Mysteries

Native American Monuments

Brian Innes

RSVP ®
RAINTREE
STECK-VAUGHN
PUBLISHERS
A Steck-Vaughn Company

Austin, Texas

Developed by Brown Partworks
Editor: Lindsey Lowe
Designer: Joan Curtis

Raintree Steck-Vaughn Publishers Staff
Project Manager: Joyce Spicer
Editor: Pam Wells

Library of Congress Cataloging-in-Publication Data
Innes, Brian.
    Native American monuments/by Brian Innes.
        p.   cm.—(Unsolved mysteries)
    Includes bibliographical references and index.
    Summary: Describes some of the ancient sites believed to have been
made by early Indian peoples, including mounds in the northern United
States, huge stone pictures in the Southwest deserts, and pyramids in
Central America.
    ISBN 0-8172-5482-X (Hardcover)
    ISBN 0-8172-4279-1 (Softcover)
    1. Mound-builders—Juvenile literature. 2. Earthworks (Archaeology)—
Juvenile literature. 3. Indian architecture—Juvenile literature. 4. America—
Antiquities—Juvenile literature.
[1. Indians—Antiquities. 2. America—Antiquities.] I. Title. II. Series: Innes,
Brian. Unsolved mysteries.
E73.I55   1999
970.01—dc21   98-13150
                                                                            CIP
                                                                            AC

Printed and bound in the United States
1 2 3 4 5 6 7 8 9 0   WZ   02 01 00 99 98

Acknowledgments

Cover Galen Rowell/Corbis; **Page 5:** Richard A.
Cooke/Corbis; **Pages 6 and 7:** Marilyn Bridges/
Corbis; **Page 9:** Library of Congress/Corbis;
Page 11: Richard A. Cooke/Corbis; **Pages 12
and 18:** Mary Evans Picture Library; **Pages 13
and 15:** David Muench/Corbis; **Pages 17 and 20:**
Richard A. Cooke/Corbis; **Page 21:** UPI/Corbis-
Bettmann; **Page 23:** Tom Bean/Corbis;
Page 24: Marilyn Bridges/Corbis; **Page 25:** The
National Archives/Corbis; **Page 27:** Adam
Woolfitt/Corbis; **Page 29:** Roman Soumar/Corbis;
Pages 30, 31, and 35: Yann Arthus-Bertrand/
Corbis; **Page 32:** South American Pictures; **Page
34:** Gianni Dagli Orti/Corbis; **Page 36:** Associated
Press; **Pages 39, 40, and 45:** Werner Forman;
Page 42: Michael T. Sedam/Corbis; **Page 43:**
Gianni Dagli Orti/ Corbis; **Page 44:** Mary Evans
Picture Library; **Page 46:** Danny Lehman/Corbis.

Contents

Giant Animal Figures

In the late 18th century, settlers found giant animal figures in many U.S. states. But who built them and when?

In the fall of 1975, Robert Harner, a sociologist, had a strange and frightening experience. A sociologist's job is to study the development of human society. Harner was driving on U.S. Highway 73 in Adams County, Ohio, when he decided to turn off the road to visit the nearby Great Serpent Mound National Monument. He had not seen it since he was a child.

The mound is on top of a ridge. It was given its name because it is shaped like a giant snake. It is more than 1,300 feet (396 m) long, and stands some 3 feet (1 m) high. Covered with grass, it winds among the trees. Its "tail" is curled, and its "head" has a wide open mouth. The mouth is holding an oval shape like an egg.

A HAIR-RAISING EXPERIENCE

Robert Harner walked to the top of the ridge and stood on the serpent's head. He wondered why the mound was there. Suddenly, he was overcome by a sense of fear: "The coldest, most hopeless terror I have ever experienced. I felt the hair rising on the nape of my neck. I could neither move nor speak. I knew that, although I was completely alone, I was not really alone."

The Great Serpent Mound in Adams County, Ohio (opposite). It is now a National Monument and has a walkway around it.

4

"Its 'tail' is curled, and its 'head' has a wide open mouth. The mouth is holding an oval shape like an egg."

Most of the leaves had already fallen from the trees around the site. As Harner watched them, they began to move, even though there was no wind. One by one, the leaves moved toward him. When they were about 20 feet (6 m) away, they started swirling together, dancing around him.

This is one of the giant bear figures that William Pidgeon discovered on a ridge in Iowa.

Harner had a camera in his car. He forced himself to move. But even as he did so: "I saw that already the leaves were walking back down the hillside. I knew I could never get back in time to photograph them."

As he stood there in amazement, Harner realized something. He became sure that he had caught a glimpse of "a small portion of that world I did not believe existed." He thought it must have been a "spirit world" that the builders of the mound would also have known. "Perhaps," he wrote later, "they built their mound on that particular hill because very special things happen there."

EXPLAINING THE MOUNDS

The first pioneers began to arrive in Ohio in the 1780s. They were amazed to discover a number of huge mounds of earth. These were not natural parts of the landscape. The mounds had obviously been created by humans. Strangest of all, some of the mounds were shaped like animals and birds. The Great Serpent Mound is the largest, but there were many others, some of which have since disappeared. The settlers refused to believe that the mounds had been built by the woodland natives. They thought they must have been constructed by people from a more developed civilization who had since disappeared.

MAN WITH A MISSION

One man who took a great interest in these mysterious shapes was William Pidgeon. He was a trader among the Native Americans. He had also traveled in South America and had studied native culture on both continents. In 1840, Pidgeon was living near a place called Fort Ancient. This is a huge earthwork on the top of a hill overlooking the Little Miami River, about 20 miles (32 km) northeast of the city of Cincinnati, Ohio. It seems to have been built for defense. The walls are 20 feet (6 m) high in places, and altogether about 4 miles (6.5 km) in length.

Pidgeon was sure that Fort Ancient had been built by people from a vanished civilization. He wanted to learn more, so he set off in a small boat to travel along the network of creeks and small lakes to the south and west of Lake Michigan. Through the woods and on the hills, Pidgeon found a whole zoo of animal mounds. He saw lizards, falcons, mountain lions, and turtles, and on

An eagle mound in a forest in Georgia. William Pidgeon found many similar mounds during his travels in the 1840s.

a ridge in Iowa he discovered a complete line of enormous bears. At a trading post on the upper Mississippi, Pidgeon met an old Native American man named De-coo-dah. He told Pidgeon that "The face of the earth is the [American Indian's] book, and those mounds and embankments are some of his letters." De-coo-dah then went on to explain this.

Many animal gods, including serpents, had been worshiped in the past. But there was war among the Native American nations, and many worshipers of serpents were killed. The survivors were forced to recognize the Sun, Moon, and other objects in the solar system as their gods. De-coo-dah said that as a result of this, the defeated native tribes had secretly built the mounds as a symbol of their belief in the old animal gods. They are very sacred places.

"The face of the earth is the [American Indian's] book, . . ."

DE-COO-DAH

MAPPING THE MOUNDS

Soon after William Pidgeon made his long journey, geologists began to examine the mounds in Ohio. There are as many as 10,000 in that one state alone. Many more animal mounds have been found in southern and southwestern Wisconsin, and in nearby areas of Minnesota, Iowa, and Illinois.

Some of these mounds are in the shapes of deer and buffalo, and birds are also common. The largest bird mound is near Madison, Wisconsin. It has a total wingspan of some 624 feet (190 m). There are also a number of human figures.

An engraving of the Great Mound at Marietta, Ohio, done in 1848. The settlement was founded in 1788, the date Manasseh Cutler visited the site.

In 1881, Theodore Lewis and Alfred Hill decided to map the mounds found in the Mississippi Valley. In 1892, Lewis and Hill produced a map that included what is now the Effigy Mounds National Monument in Iowa. This National Monument was set up on August 10, 1949, to save some of the earth mounds that had been found in northeastern Iowa. Inside its boundary are 191 known mounds. Some are huge. The Great Bear Mound is 70 feet (21 m) across the shoulders and forelegs, 137 feet (42 m) long, and over 3 feet (1 m) high.

HOW OLD ARE THE MOUNDS?

In 1788, a Massachusetts clergyman called Manasseh Cutler arrived at Marietta, on the Ohio River. He found a group of mounds. New settlers were beginning to cut down the trees on the mounds to create clearings. Cutler knew that the trees must have grown after the mounds were built, so he counted the growth rings in the tree trunks. He concluded that the mounds were at least 1,000 years old.

More recently, researchers have found that the animal mounds were built between about 400 B.C. and A.D. 1100. But why were they built? Nobody is sure, but perhaps De-coo-dah's explanation is true.

Inside the Mounds

When people began to dig into the mounds, they found bones and buried treasure.

One of the first people to examine the mysterious mounds that have been found throughout eastern America was Thomas Jefferson, who became the third President of the United States.

Sometime around 1780, while he was governor of Virginia, Jefferson decided to excavate a small mound near his home. When he dug into it, he found that it was full of human bones. It looked as if they had just been "emptied . . . from a bag or basket," he wrote. Altogether, Jefferson thought that the mound contained as many as 1,000 skeletons. It was a burial site.

BURIED TREASURE

Other people dug into similar mounds. In addition to finding bones, they discovered pottery, tools, ornaments, and simple weapons. At Grave Creek, in West Virginia, there is a cone-shaped mound almost 70 feet (21 m) high. It measures 240 feet (73 m) across. In 1838, it was known as the Mammoth Mound. The owner, named Abelard Tomlinson, dug into it. He found two tombs made from logs. They contained human bones, as well as ornaments made from mica (which is a type of mineral), shell, and copper.

This beautiful mica hand (opposite) was found inside one of the ancient burial mounds in Ohio.

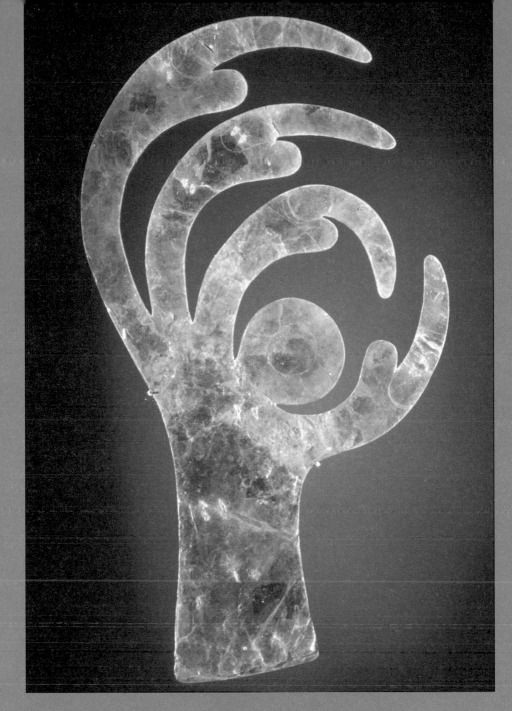

"They contained many human bones, as well as ornaments made from mica."

However, Tomlinson also claimed to have found a small piece of sandstone. It seemed to have writing on it. For many years, experts tried to figure out what the writing said. In the end, they decided that the writing was a hoax.

At Circleville, 20 miles (32 km) south of Columbus, in Ohio, a settlement had been built on top of a square earthwork. Beside it were two circular earthworks, one inside the other. The local postmaster, Caleb Atwater, decided to study these mounds and those in the neighboring states. He published his findings in 1820.

Human remains were discovered in many of the burial mounds. This is a 19th-century drawing of a mound in Ohio. However, in the 20th century, laws were passed to prevent such disturbance of sacred Native American ground.

Atwater made many interesting claims. He said that the mounds had been built by people from faraway India. He thought that a pot found in Tennessee proved this. It was shaped like a three-headed god that was worshiped in India.

OTHER MOUND STUDIES

One man who puzzled over the mounds in these early years was the physician Samuel G. Morton. In 1839, he published his studies of nearly 1,000 skulls found buried in the mounds. He divided them into two groups. One was from the Native Americans, who lived north of present-day Mexico. But the other group, he suggested, came from the Toltecs, an ancient native people who had lived in Mexico.

Not far south of Circleville is the town of Chillicothe. From 1845 to 1847, newspaper editor Ephraim G. Squier and physician Edwin H. Davis explored more than 200 mounds and 100 earthworks in the area. They made careful excavations of Mound City, a group of 23 mounds containing many skeletons. They also described the pottery, ornaments, and other objects they found and made detailed drawings. Their work is still of great value, because many mounds have since disappeared. Many have been destroyed by farmers plowing over them.

RELIGIOUS PURPOSE

Squier and Davis decided that the earthworks were "sacred enclosures." They said they had a religious purpose. They guessed that the builders had a good knowledge of math and engineering. And Squier thought that the earthworks required "a degree of knowledge much superior to that . . . possessed by the hunter tribes of North America." Most people agreed with Squier.

In 1873, J. W. Foster, president of the Chicago Academy of Sciences, wrote that to believe the mounds had been built by the Native Americans was "as preposterous as to suppose that they built the pyramids of Egypt."

Eventually, in 1881, Congress approved the sum of $5,000 for a full-scale scientific study.

This model is of the Mound City Group National Monument near Chillicothe, Ohio. The area was first mapped by Squier and Davis between 1845 and 1847.

13

Who Built the Mounds?

In the 19th century, some of the secrets of the great mounds were finally revealed.

Many of the great mounds were finally shown to have been Native American burial sites. Religious ceremonies, like the museum view shown here, were held in temples on top of some sites.

The man behind the first scientific investigation of the mounds was John Wesley Powell. He was interested in the Native American tribes. In 1879 he persuaded the Smithsonian Institution to set up a special department. Its job was to study humans, their races, and where they came from. Powell was appointed chief of the department and held this post until his death in 1902.

In 1881, Powell instructed a member of his team, Cyrus Thomas, to answer the question, "Were the mounds built by Indians?"

WORKING AGAINST TIME

Many mounds had already been destroyed, so Thomas knew he had to work fast. He selected a number of important mounds in several different areas and had them all investigated at the same time. In less than four years, Thomas and his assistants looked at 2,000 mounds in 24 different states. They found about 40,000 artifacts, or objects made by human hand.

Thomas published his report in 1894. It was 730 pages long. He showed that the different types of mounds had been built by different cultures at different times. But they were all Native

"He is in the country of the spirits, and in two days I will go to join him . . . ."

TATTOOED SERPENT'S WIFE

Americans. In the southeast, mound building had continued even after the arrival of European settlers. Thomas concluded that: "The links directly connecting the Indians and the mound builders are so numerous . . . that there should no longer be any hesitancy in [doubt about] accepting the theory that they are one and the same people."

In the last 100 years, archaeologists have gradually pieced together the history of the Mound Builders. They have divided them into three distinct cultures.

THE ADENA PEOPLE

The earliest culture is known as the Adena. It was named after a mound near Chillicothe, Ohio, which was dug up in 1901. Most of the Adena mounds occur within 150 miles (241 km) of Chillicothe and the Scioto River. But they are also found throughout western Pennsylvania, West Virginia, northern Kentucky, and southeastern Indiana.

The Adena seem to have begun building mounds around 500 B.C. They were used as burial places. At first, the Adena dug a shallow pit for the body and heaped dirt of different colors into a low mound. The different colors gave it a patchwork appearance. Nobody knows why they did this. Later, they built tombs of logs and covered them with earth. Over the years, more bodies were added, making the mound ever higher. In 1958, the skeletons of at least 54 bodies in three layers were found in the Cresap Mound in West Virginia.

The layers of the mound showed how the Adena developed their skills over the centuries. At the bottom were chipped stone tools and bone needles. Later levels contained bracelets and rings made from copper. There were also ornaments made from very thin sheets of the mineral mica. The top layer always contained what is called a trophy skull. This either belonged to a conquered enemy, or to an important ancestor. It was laid in the lap of one of the skeletons.

Other mounds have produced objects that would have belonged to shamans, or "medicine men." There was a headdress made from the skull and antlers of an elk. There were the jawbones of wolves, shaped so that they could be held in a human mouth. These would have been used in religious ceremonies. The Great Serpent Mound in Ohio is thought to be the biggest of the Adena mounds.

THE HOPEWELL

Around 100 B.C., the Adena culture gave way to the Hopewell. Their culture spread out over a wide area, east of the Great Plains. The Hopewell traveled by river, as far north as the Great Lakes and northern

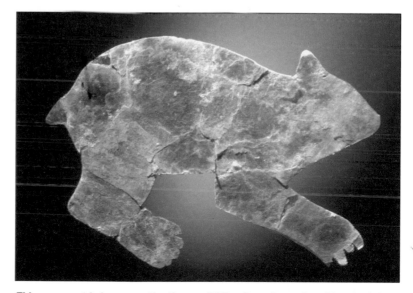

This ornament is known as the Hopewell Mica Bear. It was found in a burial mound in Ohio. It is shaped like some of the animal mounds found in Iowa.

Ontario. They were searching for copper and silver. Southward, they reached Florida and the Gulf Coast. From there, they brought tortoise shells, barracuda jaws, conch shells, and alligator teeth. They made these into ornaments and jewelry.

The Hopewell are named after a farm in Ohio, where about 30 mounds were found. These mounds seem to have been built for religious ceremonies. They were grouped to form precise squares and long avenues. About 100 years ago, half the mounds on the Hopewell farm were dug up. There were 48 skeletons in the largest mound. The artifacts found in the mounds were put on show at the World's Columbia Exposition, which was a great exhibition held in Chicago, Illinois, in 1893. On display were copper fish and birds, and a headdress like a deer's antlers, made from copper-covered wood. There were also ornaments and jewelry made from mica.

This painting shows Chicago during the World's Columbia Exposition in 1893. Many objects from the Hopewell mounds were on display for the first time.

Thirty years later, an archaeologist found the skeletons of a young man and woman in the same mound. They were laid side by side. The young woman's body was wrapped with thousands of pearl beads. She wore copper bracelets, and both skeletons had copper ear ornaments, necklaces of grizzly bear teeth, and copper breastplates.

"These mounds seem to have been built for religious ceremonies."

The Hopewell valued pearls, which came from freshwater mussels in the nearby rivers. The mounds at the Hopewell farm contained some 100,000 pearls. A single grave in another mound in Ohio contained 12,000 pearls, 35,000 pearl beads, and 20,000 shell beads. However, although the contents of the mounds reveal something of the Hopewell way of life, they do not explain the meaning of the huge geometric shapes.

SCHOOL OF MATHEMATICS

James A. Marshall, a civil engineer in Illinois, surveyed more than 200 sites. He concluded that the Hopewell had a "school of mathematics." They knew about the forms of geometry. They appeared to have first made a model of the mound. Then they marked its shape on the ground before digging.

The work involved was immense. The mound site at Newark, Ohio, once covered more than 4 square miles (10 square km). It has been suggested that its construction must have taken about 300 years!

THE MISSISSIPPIANS

Around A.D. 400, the Hopewell culture began to decline. In their place came a group of people who have been named the Mississippians. Archaeologists have discovered that the Mississippians grew better corn than those people who lived before them. As a result, their way of life was easier.

Many of the mounds are in the valley of the Mississippi River, from which the culture gets its name. The Mississippians built flat-topped pyramids, from 18 to 60 feet (5.5 to 18 m) high. Temples were built on the tops. The greatest of all the Mississippian sites is the Cahokia Mound group. These mounds were once clustered over several square miles in the Mississippi Valley, east of St. Louis, Missouri. In all, about 200 mounds were built there from A.D. 700 to 1500. Monk's Mound, the largest in the complex, is 100 feet (30.5 m) high and covers about 16 acres (6.5 hectares). The Cahokia Mounds are listed as a national historic landmark.

The Mississippians built mounds that looked like flat-topped pyramids. This is Monk's Mound, the largest mound found in the Cahokia group.

In 1972, archaeologists digging near Monk's Mound, in the Cahokia Mounds State Park, uncovered what turned out to be a Native American garbage dump.

The Mississippians built mounds until the middle of the 16th century. The Spanish explorer Hernando de Soto actually watched a huge mound being enlarged in what is now Arkansas.

In the mid-1720s, a Dutch settler named Antoine Le Page du Pratz went to live with the Native American Natchez nation in Mississippi. He stayed with them for eight years and wrote about some of the religious ceremonies that took place on top of the mounds.

A BETTER PLACE

The ruler of the Natchez was called the Great Sun. He was thought to be a relative of the Sun itself. His war chief was his brother, Tattooed Serpent. Du Pratz saw the funeral of Tattooed Serpent. The body was put on display in the temple on top of a mound. Members of his household were led into the temple. They lay down on mats, and cords were put around their necks. Then they were strangled. Du Pratz was horrified. But before her own death, Tattooed Serpent's wife told the Dutchman: "What does it matter? He is in the country of the spirits, and in two days I will go to join him. . . . We will be friends for a much longer time . . . because one does not die there again. It is always fine weather, one is never hungry, and men do not make war there anymore."

Pictures in Stone

Just as the mysteries of the mounds were finally being revealed, more strange monuments were found.

In 1923, Colonel Jerry Phillips was flying over the Mojave Desert in southern California. Not far from the Mexican border, near the small town of Blythe, he saw an amazing sight. Stretching across the desert floor were the huge figures of a man and an animal with a long tail. And there were more.

At that time, these desert areas north of Yuma, on the California–Arizona state line, were almost unexplored. In fact, it is only since the 1970s that the gigantic pictures have been discovered. Much of the work has been carried out by a Californian archaeologist, Jay von Werlhof, and a local farmer, Harry Casey. They have discovered more than 275 figures. "It's absolutely addictive," Casey said. "The more you learn, the more you want to know."

EXCITING DISCOVERIES

This picture in stone (opposite) is a medicine wheel. It was found in the Coconino National Forest, near Schnebly Hill in Arizona.

The desert rocks along the lower Colorado valley are dark and shiny. The pictures have been made either by moving rocks to expose the lighter ground beneath, or by putting different-colored stones next to each other. One figure, discovered in July 1984, is of a fisherman. He

"Some of the desert markings may date back 10,000 years."

seems to be dancing on the surface of some water and aiming a spear at two fish. The spear's tip is made from hundreds of pieces of shiny quartz.

Archaeologists believe that the Mojave figures were produced over a timespan of more than 4,000 years. The oldest are thought to date back to 3000 B.C., but some are only two or three centuries old. For example, there is a figure of a horse near Yuma. The horse was unknown in these regions until a party of Spanish explorers rode through in 1540. The images of the man and animal found near Blythe may be only 200 years old, but some scientists think they could be 1,000 years old.

MOJAVE LEGENDS

Von Werlhof and other archaeologists believe that the figures had a symbolic meaning for the Mojave Indians, who have lived in the region for more than 5,000 years. The Mojave legends give an explanation for the Blythe figures. An evil giant is said to have terrorized their ancestors. This is the huge human figure, thought to be called Ha-ak. The animal above its head is a mountain lion, a symbol of great power. It was put there to weaken the strength of the giant.

The huge figures in the desert near Blythe. The human is said to be Ha-ak, a child-eating giant. The animal is thought to be Numeta, a mountain lion.

Some of the desert markings may date back 10,000 years. These are lines of rocks in patterns of simple shapes. It is possible that these rocks were put in place by ancient astronomers.

These people would have studied the movement of objects in the sky. For example, a line of rocks along the Gila River, which runs into the Colorado River at Yuma, Arizona, points precisely toward sunrise around the date of the

These two Mojave men were photographed on the banks of the Colorado River in 1871.

summer solstice, June 22. Another rock pattern is known as the Black Point Dance Circle. It seems to be a map of the Sun, the Moon, and the broad band of hazy stars that is known as the Milky Way.

MEDICINE WHEELS

Elsewhere across the U.S. and in Canada, too, people have discovered another type of stone picture. This is in the form of a big wheel with spokes. A famous one was found on a windy plateau, high up in the Bighorn Mountains of Wyoming. Others have been found in Saskatchewan, Canada; in Arizona; and in about 50 other places. They are all on high ground. Some are only a few feet across, while others are hundreds of feet wide. They are known as medicine wheels and are considered to be sacred.

All the medicine wheels are made very simply. Stones are piled into very narrow lines, to make a wheel hub, rim, and a number of spokes—like a simple drawing of a bike wheel, for example. Some have special piles of stones a little higher than the rest, at the center, or at points along the rim. These piles of stones are called "cairns."

"It is possible that these rocks were put in position by ancient astronomers."

The Bighorn medicine wheel is in the best condition. Few of the stones have been disturbed. The wheel is 82 feet (25 m) across. On the southwest side of the wheel, just beyond the rim, is a ring-shaped cairn. It is joined to the wheel by a line of stones. This is in a straight line with one of the spokes, leading to the hub of the wheel. Anybody who stands over the cairn, looking along this line, will see the Sun rising over a distant ridge on the morning of the summer solstice. Other cairns point to the rising and setting of certain particularly bright stars.

OTHER STONE CIRCLES

Some archaeologists have compared the medicine wheels to the huge circles of upright stones (called megaliths) that are found in Western Europe. It is believed that these, also, were places where people observed the Sun, Moon, and other happenings in the skies. The most famous of them is Stonehenge, in southern England. Some of the medicine wheel

Stonehenge casts shadows across Salisbury Plain, in England. The standing stones were put up over a period of 1,500 years, starting in about 3000 B.C.

cairns cover holes that seem to have held wooden posts at one time. If this is so, the wheels would once have looked like a wooden version of Stonehenge.

Experts think that the medicine wheels were made by the Plains tribespeople about 1,000 years ago. But nobody knows why they needed to watch the skies so carefully. Agricultural peoples need to know the changing of the seasons so they can plant their crops. But the Plains nations were nomads. That is, they traveled from place to place, following the herds of buffalo that provided their food. We can only guess that the rising of the Sun on the longest day, and the movement of the bright stars, had a religious importance. The discovery of the most remarkable stone pictures in the world, made thousands of miles away in Peru, seems to support this theory.

Signals to the Gods?

Were the stone pictures of North America and the strange drawings in Peru messages to another world?

In 1941, American historian Paul Kosok and his wife, Rose, traveled to southern Peru. They went to study the ditches and waterways that the ancient peoples had dug to irrigate their crops. But on the high plateau of Nazca, they found an extraordinary sight.

Stretching across the desert were hundreds of lines scratched in the dirt. Some came from a central point, like the spokes of a wheel. Others led to huge shapes made from straight lines or curves. Some of them looked like airport runways. The local people called these the "Inca roads." The Inca civilization had existed in South America from around A.D. 1200 to 1533.

KEY TO THE RIDDLE?

Kosok and his wife drove up to a high, flat area. "We found not only many more lines," wrote Kosok, "but also two huge rectangles. . . . Most amazing of all, we found, adjacent to [next to] one of the rectangles, and close to the original center, the faint remains of a huge, peculiar pebble and dirt drawing, over 150 feet (45 m) long." Standing right at the center of the markings, the Kosoks watched the dramatic sunset.

In the early 1940s, hundreds of lines and many huge drawings (opposite) were found stretching out across the surface of Peru's Nazca Desert.

**"Most spectacular of all
is the huge drawing on
a hillside overlooking
Pisco Bay. . . ."**

This photograph of a pattern of lines in the Nazca Desert was taken from a plane about 30 years after they were first discovered by Paul and Rose Kosok.

"We suddenly noticed that it was setting almost exactly over the end of one of the long single lines! A moment later we recalled that it was June 22, the day of the winter solstice in the Southern Hemisphere—the shortest day in the year. . . . With a great thrill we realized at once that we had apparently found the key to the riddle."

Kosok thought that the lines—like the medicine wheels found in North America, or the stone circles of Europe—were probably places where ancient peoples had observed the Sun, the Moon, and other happenings in the skies.

SECRETS OF NAZCA

Huge drawings of animals were also found on the Nazca plateau. They were formed in a similar way to those in the Mojave Desert. The Nazca Desert is made from yellowish, sandy clay. This is covered with a layer of black rocks. The drawings were made by scraping the rocks to one side to show the paler earth.

The giant figures are of many different kinds. There is a spider 150 feet (45 m) long. There are 18 bird figures. One of these is a carefully drawn hummingbird. Its beak, which is 120 feet (36 m) long, points directly at sunrise on the day of the winter solstice. The Nazca lands are dry and barren. However, there are also drawings of water animals—a cormorant, a duck, a frog, and a whale.

Most spectacular of all is the huge drawing on a hillside overlooking Pisco Bay, 130 miles (209 km) north of Nazca. It is nearly 600 feet (183 km) long, and is known as the Candelabra. It could, indeed, be a three-branched candlestick, but experts cannot agree on what it represents.

At the end of the summer of 1941, Paul Kosok had to get back to teaching his classes at Long Island University. However, before he left Peru, he met a

This amazing drawing of a giant spider is only seen clearly from the air. But how could the ancient peoples who drew it see what it looked like at ground level?

In the late 1940s, Maria Reiche viewed the huge drawings in the Nazca Desert from a dangerous position on a stepladder.

woman in Lima, the capital city of Peru. Kosok told her all about his discoveries.

This woman was Maria Reiche. Born in Germany, she had studied math at the Hamburg University during the 1920s. By 1941, she was in Lima working as a teacher and as a translator of scientific texts.

Kosok asked Maria Reiche to take a look at the Nazca lines and figures. She was to spend the rest of her life studying them. In 1945, Reiche moved from Lima to a town near the Nazca plateau. She began to make detailed maps of the area. To see the complete drawings, she had to stand on a high stepladder.

DAY AND NIGHT

For weeks on end, Reiche camped out in the desert. She found lines that pointed to the Sun, Moon, and stars on important dates. These included sunrise and sunset at the summer and winter solstices, and at the spring and fall equinoxes (the two days of the year when day and night are the same length). Lines also marked the appearance of stars over the horizon.

Maria Reiche wrote that what she found most impressive about the drawings was their accuracy, given their enormous size. She wondered how the ancients could have drawn the animal figures, with their beautifully laid out curves and other details. They could not have seen them correctly while they were drawing them.

SEEN FROM ABOVE

The lines and drawings can only be clearly seen from high in the air. Even when standing on her ladder, Maria Reiche had only been able to make out faint outlines in the dust.

In the 1970s, an American photographer named Marilyn Bridges took a wonderful series of photographs of the drawings. She took them from a plane, sometimes flying as low as 200 feet (61 m) over the desert. She took most of her pictures in the early morning or early evening, because the light at these times threw shadows that made the figures stand out more clearly.

"She found lines that pointed to the Sun, Moon, and stars on important dates."

As Reiche discovered more and more animal figures, she noted that they were similar to figures found on the pottery and textiles of the Nazcan tribes. Little is known about these people, but they are known to have lived in southern Peru from 300 B.C. to A.D. 540, before the Inca empire.

This is a piece of cloth made by the Nazcan people. Maria Reiche said these pictures were similar to the drawings in the desert.

SIGNALS TO THE GODS?

So what were these drawings for? In 1968, a Swiss hotel manager called Erich von Däniken announced his theories in a book, *Chariots of the Gods?* He suggested that the Nazca lines were runways for alien spaceships. At the ends of some of the lines were mysterious "burn pits." These were some 30 to 40 feet (9 to 12 m) across, filled with rocks that had been blackened by intense heat. Were they the sites where the alien rockets had taken off again? Von Däniken said the Nazcans would have seen the visiting aliens as gods. Were their giant figures meant to be signals to the gods, asking them to return?

34

Von Däniken's theory does not hold up under close examination. If aliens had arrived in the desert in rocket spaceships, they would not have needed runways. And as Maria Reiche said: "Once you remove the stones, the ground is quite soft. I'm afraid the spacemen would have gotten stuck!"

This huge line drawing of an "astronaut" was found on one of the so-called "Inca roads." Was it a signal to alien spaceships?

FLIGHTS OF FANCY

However, Reiche did also point out that the Nazcan tribes could not have seen these figures in the sand "unless they were able to fly."

Bill Spohrer, who was an American living in Peru and a member of the International Explorers' Society, was struck by this remark. In 1973, Spohrer got together with another member of the Society. He was Jim Woodman, an airline executive. They began to look for evidence. Some Nazcan pottery and cloth seemed to show men flying, as well as what appeared

35

to be balloons and kites. There was an ancient Inca legend about a boy named Antarqui, who helped the Incas in battle by flying over the enemy and reporting where they were. And then there was the story of a man named Bartolomeu da Gusmão. Gusmão was a priest, born and raised in Brazil. It was said that in 1709 he had flown a model hot-air balloon in front of the Portuguese court in Lisbon.

Spohrer and Woodman wondered whether the Native South Americans might have had a similar type of flying machine. They examined four pieces of Nazcan cloth from a burial site. They found that the cloth was tightly woven. It was certainly good enough for a hot-air balloon. Perhaps the "burn pits" had been places where a fire was lit to heat the air for the balloon. The two men decided to test their theory.

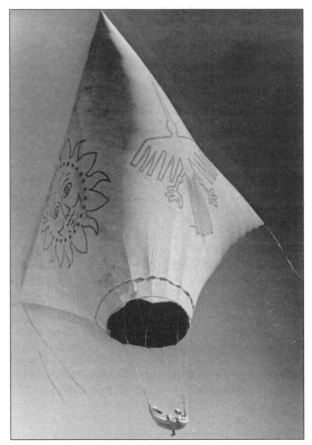

FLIGHT OF CONDOR

The hot-air balloon, *Condor I*, was built in South Dakota. It was made from a modern cotton fabric, with a weave that was similar in weight to the Nazcan cloth.

Condor 1 *flies! The balloon was decorated with drawings of the sun and a hummingbird. These were copied from the images that had been found in the dirt of the desert.*

The balloon was like an upside-down pyramid. When it was filled with air, it was 88 feet (27 m) high. Underneath hung a banana-shaped gondola woven from reeds cut on the shores of Lake Titicaca, which is on the border between Peru and Bolivia.

"Surely, I thought, the men who created these lines had to have seen them like this."

JIM WOODMAN

At the end of November 1975, a team of 30 people gathered in the Nazca Desert. Woodman and his copilot, British ballooning champion Julian Nott, climbed into the gondola. Within seconds, *Condor I* soared 400 feet (122 m) above the desert. Woodman later described his experience: "The sun had just cleared the mountains and now flooded the fantastic scene below. As we hung there, drifting slightly to the northwest, I was astonished to see a long Nazca runway perhaps 300 yards [274 m] off . . . several ancient lines stood out clearly in the morning sun. Surely, I thought, the men who created these lines had to have seen them like this."

Condor I flew for only 14 minutes, but Woodman had proved that the Nazcans could have built hot-air balloons. Legend has it that dying Nazcan chiefs were sent on their last journey, to the Sun, in balloons that were black. Perhaps the figures on the ground were symbols of the life of each chief—the last things he saw on his voyage to the afterlife. But the purpose of the long, straight lines remains a mystery.

The Pyramid Builders

The Native Americans of Mexico and Central America built great stone pyramids to honor their gods.

This mask of a jaguar holding a god in its mouth (opposite) was found in an Olmec pyramid in Mexico. The jaguar was a powerful symbol to the Olmecs. Similar carvings have been found in other Olmec pyramids.

The ancient peoples of Mexico and Central America were pyramid builders. But their pyramids were very different from those of the North American Mississippians. They had raised mounds of earth, basketful by basketful. But the peoples of Mexico and Central America built their pyramids from stone slabs, and on the flat tops they built large stone temples.

The oldest civilization in this part of America was that of the Olmecs. It dates back to before 1000 B.C. It seems that the Olmecs were the first to build pyramids in Mexico, although they did not build in stone. On the Yucatán peninsula in Mexico, a huge pyramid was made from yellow clay. Inside, archaeologists found a huge jaguar mask. To the Olmecs, the jaguar was an earth monster that caused earthquakes.

CITIES OF STONE

When the Olmec civilization disappeared, it was replaced by the Maya. The Mayan people built huge stone temples from limestone. These had a central court surrounded by pyramids and smaller buildings. Tall shafts of stone, which are called steles, stood in front of the buildings.

"To the Olmecs, the jaguar was an earth monster that caused earthquakes."

The earliest known stele dates back to A.D. 292. The tallest is 35 feet (10.5 m) high. Some of the steles are plain, but most of them are carved with the figures of gods, priests, and other important people. Some are also carved with a strange form of writing. The Mayan language had an "alphabet" of more than 800 symbols, and people in modern times are still trying to figure out what most of them mean.

PIECES OF A PUZZLE

One of the puzzles about Mayan architecture is how they came to use stone. They had no metals, and their tools were made from wood, bone, and stone. Somehow, using these relatively fragile materials, they carved the limestone into delicate shapes.

Because the Mayan pyramids were built from stone slabs, they did not have smoothly sloping sides like

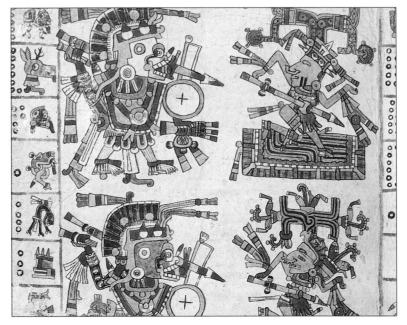

The Mayan people painted the inside walls of their buildings. This is part of a wall painting showing some of the various gods that were worshiped.

the pyramids in Egypt, or the dirt pyramids of the Mississippians. Instead, they rose on each side like a flight of steps. These were used in religious ceremonies. The priests could climb easily to the temples, while the people stood on the steps to watch.

"They could predict eclipses of the Sun and Moon and had an accurate calendar."

But what were these ceremonies? Archaeologists have been able to guess at some of them. The Maya plastered the inside walls of their buildings and then painted them. They drew scenes of ceremonial dancing and religious sacrifices. The Maya usually offered plants and animals to their gods, but some of these scenes show human sacrifices. The victim's heart would be torn out.

MANY GODS

The Maya worshiped a creator who was said to live beyond the sky. Then there was the earth mother—a strange monster that was a cross between a toad and an alligator. There were four rain gods: one for each direction—north, south, east, or west. The sky was held up by the trees and by the arms of four other gods who stood at the four points of the compass. Beneath the earth were nine underworlds. The god of death lived in the lowest underworld.

The Maya were good mathematicians. Some of the buildings they raised were used as observatories so that they could watch the skies. They could predict

The ruins of Chichén Itzá. The temple on top of the pyramid was to honor the "feathered serpent." This god was called Kukulcán by the Maya, and Quetzalcóatl by the Toltecs and Aztecs.

eclipses of the Sun and Moon and had an accurate calendar. It is possible that, as the centuries passed, this understanding of math spread northward, into North America. This might explain the accurate geometry of the Mississippians.

A NEW CIVILIZATION

Quite suddenly, around A.D. 900, the great Mayan civilization broke up. The temples were abandoned. Nobody is quite sure why, although it has been suggested that there was no rain for a long period. This would have led to temporary crop failure, and the people would have starved.

The Toltec people, who had come from the north into Mexico, gradually moved into the Mayan lands. There they built the great city of Chichén Itzá. Chichén Itzá became the most important place in the south of Mexico. The Toltecs built many temples and shrines in the Mayan style.

The Toltecs brought with them the story of Quetzalcóatl, the "feathered serpent." He was the wind god. He blew the clouds and held up the sky. Then he came to Earth as a great king. But when he set sail on a raft toward the east, the rising Sun burned him up. His blazing heart is supposed to have risen into the sky and become the planet Venus.

Quetzalcóatl became one of the most important gods of Central America. Nine Toltec kings took his name. There was a legend that Quetzalcóatl himself would one day return from the east.

THE ZAPOTECS

To the west lived the Zapotecs, around the present-day city of Oaxaca, Mexico. At Monte Albán—"the White Mountain"—the Zapotecs flattened the top of the hill into a great plateau and built a city. This was a holy place for nearly 15 centuries. There are still the remains of stepped pyramids, an observatory,

This is a modern model of tomb 104, from the Zapotec city of Monte Albán. The original tomb would probably have been for the body of a rich chief.

43

or place for observing the skies, and temples that had been built above the tombs of dead chiefs. Mitla was the last Zapotec capital. There are legends that people who were near death would go down into the chambers beneath the pyramids. They would wander there until they died. When the Aztecs arrived, they gave the place the name of Mitla, "the underworld of the dead."

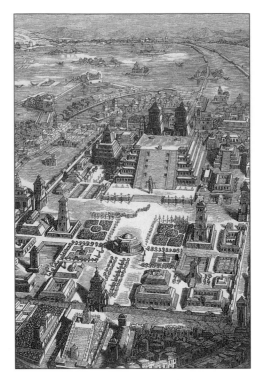

The great Aztec city of Tenochtitlán (now Mexico City). This picture shows what it would have looked like at the height of the empire's power.

AGE OF THE AZTECS

The last great civilization of Central America was the Aztec empire. But where did the Aztecs come from? Some people believe they came from California. They certainly came from the north, dressed in skins, and carrying bows and arrows. Around A.D. 1325, they settled on a group of small islands in Lake Tetzcoco. This became the city of Tenochtitlán, present-day Mexico City. From this small beginning, the Aztecs conquered the whole of Mexico, from the Atlantic to the Pacific oceans. Like the civilizations before them, the Aztecs were also pyramid builders.

The Aztec empire lasted a much shorter time than previous civilizations. In 1509, something strange happened. The emperor of the Aztecs at that time was Montezuma II. One day, his young aunt Papantzin was playing with some children. Suddenly, she fell down dead. Her body was placed in a stone coffin, ready for the funeral ceremony. Three days later, the children found Papantzin sitting in the garden. She told Montezuma II what had happened while she was "dead."

Papantzin had a vision of traveling to the shore, where she had seen great "floating houses." Men came ashore from the houses, and fought their way to Tenochtitlán. They had hairy faces, and some rode on big animals like deer without horns. The men seemed to be dressed in gray stone. They all carried shining sticks, and used them to strike down the Aztecs.

AWFUL TRUTH

Ten years later, the Spaniard Hernán Cortés arrived with his ships on the east coast of Mexico. His troops wore armor and carried swords. Some rode horses. Montezuma believed Cortés to be Quetzalcóatl, coming from the east to reclaim his kingdom. At first, he was welcomed. But by August 13, 1521, the Aztec empire had been conquered by the Spanish.

When Hernán Cortés first arrived in Mexico, he was welcomed by Montezuma. He was given many gifts, such as this turquoise ornament in the shape of a double-headed serpent.

The Spanish did all they could to destroy the Aztec culture. However, the ruins of many ancient cities remain in the jungle. This is the Mayan city of Palenque.

The Spaniards destroyed many of the temples and statues of the Aztec gods they found in them. But the pyramids of Mexico remained, until the jungle slowly grew up over them. It was 300 years before they began to be rediscovered.

UNANSWERED QUESTIONS

Archaeologists have been able to explain when and how such huge Native American monuments were built. But there are still many questions to be answered. Did the pyramid builders go northward from Mexico into the United States, or was it the other way around? Are the animal mounds and the figures in the Mojave and Nazca deserts symbols of the star groups seen in the heavens above?

Eighty-five years before Robert Harner had his strange experience at the Great Serpent Mound in Ohio, Fredric Ward Putnam had visited the site. "There seemed to come to me a picture, as of a distant time. . . . The unknown must become known."

Glossary

ancestor A member of the same family from a previous generation.

archaeologists People who study the history of the art and dwellings of past human life.

artifacts Something made by humans. Examples are ancient tools, weapons, or jewelry. These objects can belong to historic or prehistoric time periods.

astronomers People who make scientific studies of the movements of the stars and planets.

cairn A pile of stones that is put somewhere to act as a marker.

conquer To gain control over something, such as a piece of land or a country, by force. Also to achieve something that is difficult, such as climbing a mountain.

cormorant A large waterbird with a long neck and hooked beak.

culture The ideas, beliefs, art, and other characteristics of a particular civilization or social group.

earthwork A huge bank or mound of earth that has been dug.

equinox Either of the two times of year, usually around March 21 and September 23, when day and night are equal in length.

excavate To dig up something, or to uncover something by digging.

excavation The act of digging up something. Usually historical remains such as buildings or bones.

geologists Scientists who study the rock structure of the Earth.

geometry The branch of math that deals with lines, angles, and shapes such as squares and circles.

gondola A long, narrow, flat-bottomed boat with pointed ends. Used on the canals in Venice, Italy.

investigate To uncover certain facts in order to discover the reason for a particular event.

irrigate To supply water to dry land through canals.

Milky Way The pale white band that can be seen in the night sky. It is formed by millions of distant stars.

reclaim To ask for the return of something, or to take it back.

researchers People who gather information for study.

solar system The system of planets that move around the sun.

solstice The time of either the longest day of the year, around June 22, or the shortest day of the year, around December 22. Called the summer and winter solstices.

symbol Something that represents, or suggests, something else.

Index

Further Reading

Asimov, Isaac. *Astronomy in Ancient Times*, "Library of the Universe" series.
Gareth Stevens, Inc., 1995
Baquedano, Elizabeth. *Aztec, Inca, and Maya*, "Eyewitness Books." Knopf, 1993
Corbishley, Mike. *How Do We Know Where People Came From?* "How Do We
Know?" series. Raintree Steck-Vaughn, 1995
Putnam, James. *Pyramid*. Knopf Books, 1994
Shemie, Bonnie. *Mounds of Earth and Shell*, "Native Peoples" series. Simon and
Schuster Children, 1994

48